Play Lati..

All-time hits from Latin America for piano

Succès de toujours d'Amériques latine pour piano

Unvergängliche Hits aus Südamerika für Klavier

Arranged by John Kember

First Published in 1999 by Faber Music Ltd
3 Queen Square London WC1N 3AU
Cover design by Russell Stretten
Music processed by Wessex Music Services
Cover photo from South American Pictures/Tony Morrison
Printed in England by Halstan & Co Ltd

ISBN 0 571 51895 8

Contents

To buy Faber Music publications or to find out about the full range of titles available please contact you local music retailer or Faber Music sales enquiries:

Tel: +44(0) 171 833 7931
Fax: +44 (0) 171 833 7930
E-mail: sales@fabermusic.co.uk
Website: http://www.fabermusic.co.uk

Eso Beso

Words and Music by
Joe Sherman and Noel Sherman

17
2.
5
5
5
3
5
mp
21
25
mf
29
33
f
mp

37
40
43
mf
46
mp
49

Wave

Antonio Carlos Jobim

25
mf
29
34
mp
38
p
43
48
pp
Ped.

La Paloma

Sebastian Yradier

30
p
mf
36
p
mf
f
42
p
48
54
p
pp
f

La Cucaracha

Trad.

26
mp
31
36
mp
cresc. poco a poco
41
mf
cresc.
f
46
cresc.
51
ff

Mexican Hat Dance

Trad.

25
mp
30
mf
mp
35
mf
40
f
45
8

Copacabana

Words and Music by Barry Manilow,
Bruce Sussman & Jack Feldman

D.C. poi al Coda
sub. p
CODA

Cuban Serenade

John Kember

Habañera

Georges Bizet

31
5
3
4
2
5
3
4
2
f
pp
38
ten.
f
pp
ten.
3
3
44
51
f
mp
3
f
57
pp
3
f
ff

This Masquerade

Words and Music by Leon Russell

25
mf
29
f
mf
34
3
39
43
mp
48
rall.
3
3
3
3
p

La Cumparsita

Rodriguez

p
pp

36
f
p
f
39
p
f
p
42
f
mp
f
mp
46
f
mp
f
49
2
ff
1

Desafinado

Music and lyrics by
Antonio Carlos Jobim and
Newton Mendonca

17
5 3 1 3
21
2
1
mp
24
p
mf
f
28
mf
32
mp

35
mp
39
mf
42
45
poco cresc.
49
f

53
sub. p
57
mp
mf
61
65
p
mf
69
p

Meester Tango

John Kember

15
mf
19
f
mf
23
p
27
f
p
f
p
31

mf
p
mp
mf
p
mf

53
f
56
mp
60
mp
64
p
67
pp